Profiles of the Presidents

ANDREW JACKSON

★ ★ ★

Profiles of the Presidents

ANDREW JACKSON

by Barbara A. Somervill

Content Adviser: The Hermitage, Hermitage, Tennessee
Reading Adviser: Dr. Linda D. Labbo, Department of Reading Education, College of Education, The University of Georgia

COMPASS POINT BOOKS MINNEAPOLIS, MINNESOTA

Compass Point Books
3109 West 50th Street, #115
Minneapolis, MN 55410

Visit Compass Point Books on the Internet at *www.compasspointbooks.com*
or e-mail your request to *custserv@compasspointbooks.com*

Editors: E. Russell Primm, Emily J. Dolbear, Melissa McDaniel, and Catherine Neitge
Photo Researchers: Svetlana Zhurkina and Heidi Schoof
Photo Selector: Linda S. Koutris
Designer: The Design Lab
Cartographer: XNR Productions, Inc.

Library of Congress Cataloging-in-Publication Data
Somervill, Barbara A.
 Andrew Jackson / by Barbara A. Somervill.
     p. cm.— (Profiles of the presidents)
Summary: A biography of Andrew Jackson from his childhood in South Carolina, through his military career in the War of 1812, to his legacy as the seventh president of the United States. Includes bibliographical references and index.
 ISBN 0-7565-0255-1 (hardcover)
 1. Jackson, Andrew, 1767–1845—Juvenile literature. 2. Presidents—United States—Biography—Juvenile literature. [1. Jackson, Andrew, 1767–1845. 2. Presidents.] I. Title. II. Series.
 E382 .S695 2003
 973.5'6'092—dc21   2002009941

Table of Contents

★ ★ ★

*NOTE: In this book, words that are defined in the glossary are in **bold** the first time they appear in the text.*

The Frontier President

★ ★ ★

Andrew Jackson was the first "people's" president. Jackson believed that a government should represent all its citizens, not just the wealthy. He said, "In general, the great can protect themselves, but the poor and humble require the arm and shield of the law."

Jackson was the first president to be born a common man. Unlike earlier presidents, Jackson did not have wealthy parents, a university education, or family power. He was a self-made man.

Andrew Jackson believed that every U.S. citizen should have access to the White House and the country's president. No guards blocked White House doors. No rules kept strangers from coming up to shake his hand.

As president, Jackson believed he was the only person who could truly represent all the American people. He showed his authority when he vetoed, or rejected,

◄ Andrew Jackson *by artist Thomas Sully*

proposed laws. He used the veto as a way to direct national policy. He was able to control government spending by vetoing some programs passed by Congress. He did not think that the federal government should pay for projects that would not help the whole nation. Because of Jackson's action, in 1835 the U.S. government was out of debt for the first and only time in its history. Andrew Jackson was a powerful president. He was a model for the presidents who followed him.

The White House ▶
in 1825

From Brawler to Lawyer

★　★　★

Andrew Jackson was born on March 15, 1767, in the Waxhaws, an area on the border between North Carolina and South Carolina. Jackson's father, who was also named Andrew, died a few weeks before his birth. His

◄ Jackson was a common man born in a simple house like this.

death left Andrew's mother, Elizabeth, penniless. She moved in with her sister's family to provide a home for Andrew and his older brothers, Hugh and Robert.

As a child, Andrew showed more interest in riding, shooting, and fighting than in reading, writing, and arithmetic. Schoolmates and teachers said that he was a brawler, a bully, and full of mischief. Elizabeth Jackson hoped Andrew would become a minister, but her son proved more able with his fists than his books. Jackson, however, did enjoy writing. Despite his reputation for getting in trouble at school, Andrew had a fairly good education for the time.

In 1775, the Revolutionary War (1775–1783) was raging, as Americans tried to gain their independence from Great Britain. By 1780, the war had come to the Waxhaws. British soldiers poured over the region, killing 113 American soldiers in what was called the Waxhaw Massacre. The Jacksons cared for American soldiers who had been wounded. Although Andrew Jackson was only thirteen years old, he decided to join the fight. He signed up with the army and served as a messenger.

The following year, British troops captured Jackson and his brother Robert. A British officer demanded that

◄ *Andrew Jackson (right) witnessing the Waxhaw Massacre*

Andrew polish the officer's boots. When Andrew refused, the officer slashed his face with a sword. This left a scar on Jackson's forehead, which fueled his hatred of the British.

This incident left ► Jackson with a facial scar and a lifelong hatred of the British.

The Revolutionary War was disastrous for the Jackson family. Hugh died after being out in the heat too long during the battle of Stono Ferry in 1779. Robert died from the deadly disease smallpox in 1781. A few months after Robert's death, Elizabeth Jackson died from a disease called cholera while caring for wounded American soldiers. At fourteen years old, Andrew Jackson found himself without a family. He was alone in the world.

Andrew's teenage years were spent moving from one relative's home to another. Finally, he and some other rowdy young people ran away. He spent his time drinking, gambling, and horse racing. By 1784, Andrew decided that he needed a better life. He headed to Salisbury, North Carolina, to become a lawyer.

For two years, Jackson studied law with Spruce Macay. After that, he worked with Colonel John Stokes, one of the best lawyers in North Carolina. In 1787, Jackson passed a test to become a lawyer himself.

▾ *Spruce Macay's law office in Salisbury, North Carolina*

Jackson headed west to the untamed **frontier** of what is now Tennessee. The other pioneers in Tennessee needed lawyers to help them settle disputes over land, cattle ownership, and matters of honor. At that time, **duels** were also a common way of resolving personal disputes. Insults to a man's pride were settled at gunpoint.

Jackson moved to Nashville, where he lived with the Donelson family. By age twenty-five, he had become the territory's attorney general, or main legal official.

A pioneer cabin in ▼ Cades Cove, Smoky Mountains National Park, Tennessee

Jackson fell in love with the Donelsons' daughter, Rachel Donelson Robards, who was living with her parents for a time. Unfortunately, Rachel was already married to a man named Lewis Robards, but the two did not get along.

◀ *Rachel Donelson Robards*

When Lewis Robards came back to Nashville, Rachel refused to return to their home with him. Lewis filed for a divorce from Rachel. This was a rare event in the 1790s. Jackson believed that Rachel was free from her husband, so he married her and they returned to Nashville.

The divorce had never actually been granted, however. The Jacksons were shocked when they discovered this. Jackson married Rachel in 1791, but her divorce from Robards wasn't final until 1793. Rachel had committed bigamy—marriage to two people at the same time. The Jacksons married again in 1794. Years later, during the presidential election of 1828, Jackson's enemies would bring up the bigamy. Jackson defended Rachel, threatening to duel with anyone who spoke against her. Even though Jackson was an excellent shot, Rachel's first marriage would still come up in that campaign.

A view down the ▾ barrels of Jackson's dueling pistols, which were on display in a museum in this 1926 photo

In the 1790s, Tennessee was growing and thriving. Settlers poured into the area. This forced Native Americans in the region to struggle to keep their land.

▲ *Settlers fighting Native Americans for land in the Tennessee territory*

Andrew Jackson ▶
in uniform

Jackson joined the local militia, an army of part-time soldiers. He and the other militiamen were ready to protect the land for white settlers.

The population of Tennessee grew from 36,000 in 1790 to more than 60,000 by 1796. On June 1, 1796, Tennessee became the sixteenth state. It joined the Union as a state that allowed slavery. Jackson himself owned slaves who worked on his **plantation,** called Hunter's Hill.

The year Tennessee became a state, Jackson became Tennessee's first member of the House of Representatives. He headed for Philadelphia, Pennsylvania, which was then the nation's capital, to attend Congress. Rachel stayed home to manage the farm. Jackson did not plan to stay in politics, but when one of Tennessee's U.S. Senate seats opened up in 1797, Jackson was elected a senator.

Jackson was not a successful congressman. He did not have the patience for it. He had a fiery temper, and he was not a good public speaker. President Thomas Jefferson once described Jackson as a man who "could never speak on account of the rashness of his feelings. I have seen him attempt it repeatedly,

Thomas Jefferson ▲
believed Jackson's
temper affected
his success as
a politician.

and as often choke with rage."

Jackson returned home, where he was appointed to the Tennessee Supreme Court. He earned a name as a tough but honest judge. One story claimed that a thug named Russell Bean came before Jackson's court. Bean cursed the judge and jury, and then charged out of the court. Jackson sent the sheriff to bring Bean back, but the lawman returned empty-handed. Bean had threatened to shoot the first person who came within 10 feet (3 meters) of him.

Jackson stormed out of the courthouse, gun in hand. Aiming straight at Bean, Jackson yelled, "Surrender, you infernal villain, this very minute, or I'll blow you through!" Bean gave up, and Jackson's fame grew.

A National Hero

★   ★   ★

Jackson worked as a judge for several years. He also served in the state militia, rising to the rank of major general in 1802. During that time, Jackson's plantation slipped into debt for a variety of reasons. The Jacksons sold their well

▼ *Jackson's farmhouse at the Hermitage*

established Hunter's Hill plantation and bought a nearby plantation 10 miles (16 kilometers) from Nashville, which they called the Hermitage.

There, the Jacksons lived in a two-story log farmhouse. The house made a fine home for them and the son they adopted in 1809. The Jacksons made a living by a variety of means. He ran a cotton gin, a machine that

John Sevier ▲

removes the seeds and husks from cotton. They also ran three general stores, where they sold rifles, cooking utensils, salt, coffee, cloth, tobacco, and furs. At the Hermitage, the Jacksons expanded their farm to raise cotton as their cash crop. They also raised corn and wheat, along with horses, cattle, and mules.

Although Jackson had become a successful businessman, he was still quick-tempered, high-spirited, and always ready to defend his honor. Once, Jackson accused former governor John Sevier of fraud. Sevier insulted him back. True to his nature, Jackson challenged Sevier to a duel, but instead they traded curses rather than bullets. In 1806, Jackson gambled $5,000, a fortune then, on a horse race. Luckily, Jackson won, since he may not have had enough money to pay his debt. Another bet and an insult to Rachel resulted in a duel between Jackson and a man named Charles Dickinson. Jackson killed Dickinson, but only after Dickinson shot Jackson in the chest. Six years later, another brawl left a bullet in Jackson's shoulder.

▼ *Andrew Jackson (right) winning a duel*

Major General ▶
Jackson in 1814

Jackson may have been rash, but he also had a good mind for military strategy. He had no formal army training, but his military plans usually succeeded. When the United States entered a war against Great Britain called the War of 1812 (1812–1814), General Andrew Jackson was ready to serve his country.

Early in the war, a group of Creek Indians attacked white settlers who were taking over Creek land. It was an ideal time for the Native Americans to rebel, since the U.S. Army was busy fighting the British. The Red Stick Creeks, who were named for the red war clubs they carried, swept across Alabama. They killed white settlers, burned forts, and destroyed crops. General Andrew Jackson was ordered to control the Creeks. Jackson's men chased the Red Stick Creeks clear across Alabama in what was called the Creek War.

The Creek War ended at the Battle of Horseshoe Bend on March 27, 1814. Of the 1,000 Creeks fighting against Jackson's army, 557 died. Between 250 and 300 others drowned or were shot trying to cross the river. In a letter to Major General Pinckney, Jackson said, "The power of the Creeks is I think forever broken."

The Creek Indians nicknamed Jackson "Sharpknife" after their experiences with him during battles.

Because of Jackson's warlike nature, the native people called him "Sharpknife." During the Creek War, Jackson's men nicknamed him "Old Hickory." They called him this because he was as tough as hickory, a famously hard wood.

Late in 1814, President James Madison ordered Jackson to lead troops against the British, who planned to take over New Orleans, Louisiana. Before the battle started, British and American leaders signed a **treaty** to end the war. No one in New Orleans, however, knew that the war was almost over.

The British advanced, taking land south of New Orleans. They sank U.S. ships and believed they could easily beat Jackson's ragged, poorly organized troops. The

◄ *President James Madison*

British fought in traditional fashion: neat rows of soldiers and set patterns of attack.

In January of 1815, the British again attacked American troops, and both sides fought in hand-to-hand combat. The British had planned the attack poorly, however, and lost two generals. Lacking organization, they suffered one of the worst defeats of the war. In all, 700 British soldiers died in the fighting, compared to just 18 of Jackson's troops. General Jackson became a national hero. Americans knew that their independence from Britain was secure for all time. General Jackson and his men proved that the United States was strong enough to fight and win!

Jackson later turned to Florida. Some Red Stick Creeks and runaway slaves from Georgia and the Carolinas had joined with the Seminole Indians in Florida. Jackson led his men against the Seminoles, taking over Saint Marks, a town under Spanish rule, along the way in 1818. Jackson defended

Jackson's great victory over the British at the Battle of New Orleans

this by saying that townspeople were giving supplies to
the rebelling Native Americans. Jackson's troops also captured two British officers, who had trained the Seminoles
to fight against the U.S. Army. Jackson ordered both
men killed.

▲ Andrew Jackson and his troops invading Florida in 1818

　　The Spanish and British threatened war over Jackson's
actions. President Monroe stopped supporting Jackson.
Other important politicians, such as Henry Clay and
John Quincy Adams, openly criticized him.

　　By then Spain had grown tired of trying to control
Florida. It gave the region to the United States. Andrew
Jackson became the first governor of the Florida territory.
He was more popular than ever for opening new territory
to white settlers.

The Common Man's President

★ ★ ★

The 1824 election forever changed the direction of U.S. politics. It was the first time that the **candidates** publicly campaigned in an attempt to win votes. Jackson and the other presidential candidates in 1824 all belonged to the

Guests at a ball ▸ commemorating the ninth anniversary of the Battle of New Orleans include Andrew Jackson (left), Henry Clay (right), and John Quincy Adams (far right). All three became presidential opponents later that same year.

Democratic-Republican Party. John Quincy Adams, the son of former president John Adams, represented wealthy politicians. Also running were Kentucky politician Henry Clay, who had criticized Jackson over his actions in Florida, and William Crawford of Georgia.

Slogans, speeches, and political clubs became part of the election process. Finally, the election took place. When the votes were counted, Jackson had 153,544 votes; Adams, 108,740; Crawford, 46,618; and Clay, 47,136.

To become president, a candidate needed a majority—more than 50 percent—of the **electoral college** votes. In most cases at that time, the person who got the most votes in any given state won all the electoral college votes for that state. In this election, Jackson won ninety-nine electoral votes to Adams's eighty-four. Neither had the majority. No one had won the election!

▾ *John Quincy Adams*

This threw the election into the U.S. House of Representatives. The representatives would vote to decide who would be the next president. Henry Clay had won the fewest electoral college votes in the election, but he held great power in the House. People who had supported Clay switched to John Quincy

Jackson Forever!
The Hero of Two Wars and of Or'eans!
The Man of the People!
HE WHO COULD NOT BARTER NOR BARGAIN FOR THE
PRESIDENCY!

Who, although "*A Military Chieftain*," valued the purity of Elections and of the Electors, **MORE** than the Office of **PRESIDENT** itself! Although the greatest in the gift of his countrymen, and the highest in point of dignity of any in the world,

BECAUSE
It should be derived from the
PEOPLE!

No Gag Laws! No Black Cockades! No Reign of Terror! No Standing Army or Navy Officers, when under the pay of Government, to browbeat, or

KNOCK DOWN
Old Revolutionary Characters, or our Representatives while in the discharge of their duty. To the Polls then, and vote for those who will support

OLD HICKORY
AND THE ELECTORAL LAW.

An election poster supporting Andrew Jackson for president in 1828

Adams. Jackson supporters claimed that Adams and Clay had made a secret deal, which both men denied. Adams became president. He appointed Clay secretary of state.

Four years later, the election ended differently. Jackson soundly defeated President Adams, winning 647,286 votes to Adams's 508,064. Jackson received 178 electoral votes. Adams received 83. Jackson's votes represented a clear majority, so he became the people's president.

As with politics today, name-calling dirtied the campaign. In Jackson's case, supporters of the other candidate hurled insults about Rachel Jackson and her bigamy. Rachel suffered terribly from the cruel gossip. Before the election, she told a friend, "I had rather be a doorkeeper in the house of God than to live in that palace in Washington."

She got her wish. Just before Christmas 1828, Rachel died of a heart attack. Jackson blamed his political enemies for her death.

After being sworn in as president, Jackson opened the White House doors to the public. Thousands of people swarmed through the house, destroying furniture, ripping curtains, and breaking china. Even though they caused some damage, Jackson believed the White House was the people's house and that they had the right to go in.

Jackson actually did much to improve the White House during his presidency. In earlier years, the White House looked more like a barn than a real

◀ Rachel Jackson died before her husband took office.

▼ Jackson opened the White House to the public after he was sworn in.

home. During Jackson's presidency, new yellow wallpaper brightened the bare walls, and huge chandeliers lit balls and dinners. Jackson also added running water to the White House, along with a bathing room for men. Some of his political enemies said Jackson was an uncivilized westerner, but his work on the White House showed otherwise

Every president begins his term in office by choosing a **cabinet** to provide advice and support. Jackson named Martin Van Buren, who had run his election campaign, as secretary of state. His old friend John Eaton became secretary of war, while John Branch

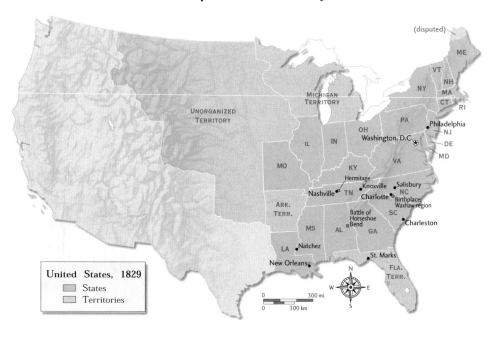

United States, 1829
- States
- Territories

became secretary of the navy. Samuel Ingham took over the treasury. John M. Berrien served as attorney general, the nation's lawyer, and William T. Barry became postmaster general.

In addition to his official advisers, Jackson also relied on a group of close political friends. This group consisted of newspaper editors Francis Blair and Amos Kendall; Maryland lawyer Roger B. Taney; and William Lewis, a political friend. These outside advisers came to be called the Kitchen Cabinet.

▾ *An 1828 celebration to mark the beginning of construction on the Baltimore and Ohio Railroad*

Jackson wanted to get the national government out of debt. He also believed that federal government money should be spent on projects that benefited the nation as a whole, not just a certain state or city. Congress wanted to pay for new canals, railroads, and highways. They passed a number of bills, or proposed laws, to provide money for these projects, but Jackson used his veto to stop much of the spending. He believed that states and private companies should build roads and canals for their own use. In time, and after some vetoes, Jackson paid off the national debt. This was the first and last time in history that the U.S. government was out of debt.

President Jackson ▼
used his veto
power to stop
government spending.

The U.S. **Constitution** gives presidents the power to veto bills. Earlier presidents had used this power when they believed a law passed by Congress was unconstitutional. Jackson vetoed bills when he thought Congress was making bad policy.

The President's Political Battles

★   ★   ★

A string of political battles kept Andrew Jackson busy during his presidency. Among the most important events during Jackson's time in office was the passage of the Indian Removal Act in 1830. This law required Native Americans to leave their homelands in the East. They would be forced to settle on land in Indian Territory (present-day Oklahoma).

▾ *A Choctaw camp*

Jackson believed that the government had a responsibility to native people. He also believed, however, that the native tribes had little hope of keeping their lands. Many Americans wanted the Indian Removal Act passed, and Jackson gave them what they wanted.

More than 4,000 ►
Native Americans
died on the Trail
of Tears.

Today, many historians view the Indian Removal Act as a shameful part of American history. Many tribes refused to leave their homelands, but they were forced to move. The U.S. Army hired people to push Native Americans westward on trains, boats, and by foot. About 17,000 Cherokee, Choctaw, Creek, and Chickasaw made the trip to Indian Territory. More than 4,000 died of disease and hunger along the way. The more than 800-mile (1,287-km) march westward is called the Trail of Tears.

Many Americans agreed with the Indian Removal Act, but Jackson did not enjoy the same support with the way he handled the Second Bank of the United States. Jackson never trusted banks and preferred to buy and sell goods with gold when he conducted business as a plantation owner.

When Jackson took office, the United States had no regular form of money. The nation's money was a mix of paper money printed by banks, and gold and silver coins from foreign countries. In 1816, Congress had agreed to the creation of the Second Bank of the United States. Wealthy private citizens owned the bank, which held all the federal government's coins and paper money. Jackson was concerned that these people, along with wealthy foreign investors, controlled the nation's money supply.

▼ Silver coins made up a part of the nation's money supply. This silver dollar, dated 1804, was actually minted in the early 1830s to give to foreign leaders.

▼ The Second Bank of the United States is located in Philadelphia.

He also wanted to make sure the policies of the Bank of the United States didn't always favor this group of upper class citizens at the expense of commen men like farmers and laborers. Jackson worried that the bank made too many decisions favoring large and wealthy companies. He believed that such policies hurt the working class citizens he has always fought so hard to protect.

The banking system also did a poor job balancing its use of gold and paper money. The Second Bank and smaller state banks each printed their own paper money, which people could turn in for gold whenever they wanted to. Soon, problems arose. People with state bank notes wanted money issued by the Second Bank. They thought the Second Bank would have enough gold to back up its paper money. As state bank notes were changed for Second Bank paper money, state bank cash piled up in the Second Bank. The Second Bank could then demand gold from the state banks in exchange for their paper money. Often, a state bank did not have enough gold, and it went bankrupt. This gave the Second Bank great power.

Secretary of the ▼
Treasury William
Duane

Jackson wanted to limit the Second Bank's power. He told a group of bankers, "You are a den of thieves. I intend to rout you out, and by the eternal God, I will rout you out." Once Jackson was reelected in 1832, he told Secretary of the Treasury

◄ Secretary of the Treasury Roger B. Taney

William Duane to remove all government money from the Second Bank. Duane refused, and Jackson replaced him with Roger B. Taney, who had been the attorney general. This was the first time a president replaced a cabinet member because of a disagreement over policy. Taney did what Jackson wanted. He took all the federal money out of the Second Bank and put it in the state banks.

Jackson's actions and the response of the banks set off a cycle of economic disaster. The Second Bank demanded gold for the state bank currency it held. State banks made more paper money—five times more paper money than the gold they held. Cotton prices fell, hurting the economy in the South. The paper money issued by the state banks proved to be worthless, and panic struck the economy. It took six years for the nation's economy to recover from Jackson's well-meant, but poorly managed, bank war.

A political cartoon showing Jackson's bank war

◀ *Vice President
John C. Calhoun*

From the time the United States was founded, politicians had argued over which rights should belong to the state governments and which to the federal government. During Jackson's first term, he and Vice President John C. Calhoun took opposite sides on this issue. Jackson thought the federal government should be strong. Calhoun believed the states should have more power. Jackson and Calhoun parted ways over the issue

The Port of Charleston ▲ of **tariffs**—taxes on imported goods—which Congress approved in 1828 and 1832.

Calhoun said that states had the right to nullify, or cancel, any law passed by the federal government. Right after the 1832 election, South Carolina passed an Ordinance of Nullification. This law canceled the 1828 and 1832 federal tariffs. It gave South Carolina the right to stop the federal government from collecting tariffs at the Port of Charleston. Jackson called this kind of disobedience to the law **treason.** He threatened to send troops to South Carolina to force the state to obey the federal tariff laws.

Calhoun encouraged South Carolina to leave the Union if this happened. Jackson, hearing this, said Calhoun "ought to be hung." In the end, South Carolina was not allowed to nullify the tariff laws. The Ordinance of Nullification, however, was the first sign that states might consider leaving the Union.

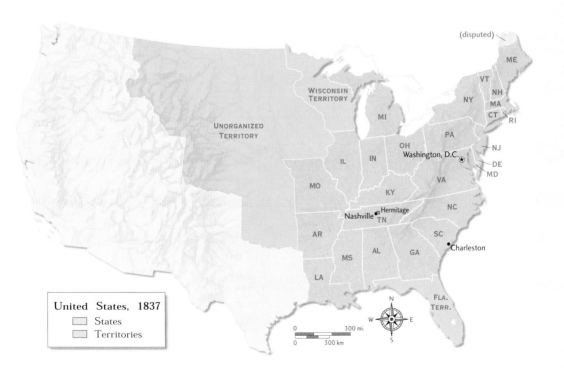

United States, 1837
- States
- Territories

Last Days at the Hermitage

★ ★ ★

Martin Van Buren, eighth president of the United States

In 1837, Jackson's political power swept Martin Van Buren into the presidency. Jackson looked forward to retirement at the Hermitage. When Van Buren was sworn in as president, Jackson said, "My own race is nearly run; advanced age and failing health warn me that before long I must pass beyond the reach of human events and cease to feel the [trials] of human affairs. . . . I bid you a last and affectionate farewell." He headed home with all of his savings—barely $90. Crowds cheered him along the route to Tennessee.

At the Hermitage, Jackson discovered that his son had not run the plantation the way Jackson had wanted. Jackson was burdened by heavy debts that he couldn't repay. Fortunately, friends helped him out. They loaned him money to pay his debts.

▼ *The Hermitage, Jackson's plantation home near Nashville, Tennessee*

Andrew ▸
Jackson, two
months before
he died

Jackson's health declined. He still suffered from the bullet wound he had received in the duel with Charles Dickinson. His lungs were also failing. He suffered from severe headaches, and he could rarely lie down comfortably.

Despite his illness, visitors called upon him daily. Jackson said, "I am dying as fast as I can, and they all know it, but they will keep swarming upon me in crowds." On June 8, 1845, Jackson died at age seventy-eight. He was buried at the Hermitage next to his wife, Rachel.

During his lifetime, Jackson changed the face of politics and government in the United States. For the first time, presidents actively campaigned for office. Jackson's frequent use of vetoes became a model for how future presidents would control lawmaking. The Kitchen Cabinet, Jackson's group of unofficial advisers, also became commonplace.

Jackson once said, "One man with courage makes a majority." Although he did not have the wealth and formal education of earlier presidents, he relied on his own bravery and determination to change a nation. Because of these things, he is the only president to have an era named for him. The Age of Jackson—the time from the War of 1812 to the Civil War (1861–1865)—stands as a monument to Andrew Jackson's belief in government by and for the common man.

The tomb of Andrew ▶ Jackson is located on the grounds of the Hermitage.

GLOSSARY

★ ★ ★

cabinet—a president's group of advisers who are heads of government departments

candidates—people running for office in an election

Constitution—the document stating the basic laws of the United States

duels—formal fights with weapons between two people, often over an insult

electoral college—a group of people who elect the U.S. president; each state is given a certain number of electoral votes; the candidate who receives the most votes from the people is awarded the state's electoral votes

frontier—the edge of settled land in a country

plantation—a large farm in the South, usually worked by slaves

slogans—phrases used to capture public attention in a campaign

tariffs—taxes placed on certain foreign goods entering a country

treason—an attempt to betray one's own country

treaty—an agreement between two governments

ANDREW JACKSON'S LIFE AT A GLANCE

★ ★ ★

PERSONAL

Nickname:	"Old Hickory"
Birth date:	March 15, 1767
Birthplace:	The Waxhaws, in the western Carolinas
Father's name:	Andrew Jackson
Mother's name:	Elizabeth Hutchinson Jackson
Education:	Little formal education
Wife's name:	Rachel Donelson Robards Jackson (1767–1828)
Married:	August 1791; second ceremony held January 17, 1794
Children:	Andrew Jackson Jr. (1801–1865)
Died:	June 8, 1845
Buried:	The Hermitage

PUBLIC

Occupations before presidency:	Lawyer, soldier, politician, farmer, storekeeper
Occupation after presidency:	Retired
Military service:	General in the War of 1812 and the Seminole Wars
Other government positions:	U.S. representative; U.S. senator; justice of the Tennessee Supreme Court; governor of Florida Territory
Political party:	Democratic-Republican; Democrat
Vice presidents:	John C. Calhoun (1829–1832); Martin Van Buren (1832–1837)
Dates in office:	March 4, 1829–March 3, 1837
Presidential opponents:	John Quincy Adams, 1828; Henry Clay, 1832
Number of votes (Electoral College):	647,286 of 1,155,350 (178 of 261), 1828; 687,502 of 1,250,799 (219 of 288), 1832
Writings:	None

★

Andrew Jackson's Cabinet

Secretary of state:
Martin Van Buren (1829–1831)
Edward Livingston (1831–1833)
Louis McLane (1833–1834)
John Forsyth (1834–1837)

Secretary of the treasury:
Samuel D. Ingham (1829–1831)
Louis McLane (1831–1833)
William J. Duane (1833)
Roger B. Taney (1833–1834)
Levi Woodbury (1834–1837)

Secretary of war:
John H. Eaton (1829–1831)
Lewis Cass (1831–1836)

Attorney general:
John M. Berrien (1829–1831)
Roger B. Taney (1831–1833)
Benjamin F. Butler (1833–1837)

Postmaster general:
William T. Barry (1829–1835)
Amos Kendall (1835–1837)

Secretary of the navy:
John Branch (1829–1831)
Levi Woodbury (1831–1834)
Mahlon Dickerson (1834–1837)

ANDREW JACKSON'S LIFE AND TIMES

★ ★ ★

JACKSON'S LIFE			WORLD EVENTS

March 15, Jackson is born in the Waxhaws, in the western Carolinas — 1767

1770 — 1770 — Five die in a street clash that becomes known as the Boston Massacre (above)

1777 — Vermont is the first former colony to ban slavery

Joins the army to fight the British in the Revolutionary War — 1780 — **1780**

1783 — American author Washington Irving is born

Moves to Salisbury, North Carolina (above), to study law — 1784

JACKSON'S LIFE

Opens his own law practice	1787
Moves to Tennessee	1788
Becomes Tennessee Territory's attorney general	1789

1790

Marries Rachel Donelson Robards (below)	1791

Marries Rachel Robards a second time after discovering that she was not legally divorced from her first husband at the time of their earlier wedding — 1794

WORLD EVENTS

1791	Austrian composer Wolfgang Amadeus Mozart (above) dies
1792	The dollar currency is introduced to America
1793	Eli Whitney invents the cotton gin
1794	The U.S. navy is established

JACKSON'S LIFE

WORLD EVENTS

Elected to the U.S. House of Representatives — 1796

Becomes a U.S. senator — 1797

Elected a judge on the Tennessee Supreme Court — 1798

1799 — Napoléon Bonaparte (above) takes control of France

1800

Shot in the chest during a duel — 1806

1807 — Robert Fulton's *Clermont* (above) is the first reliable steamship to travel between New York City and Albany

1809 — American poet and short-story writer Edgar Allen Poe is born in Boston

JACKSON'S LIFE	1810	WORLD EVENTS

1812–1814   The United States and Britain fight the War of 1812

1814 Leads an army that defeats the Creek Indians during the Creek War

1814–1815   European states meet in Vienna to redraw national borders after the Napoleonic Wars

1815 Becomes a national hero after defeating the British in the Battle of New Orleans during the War of 1812 (below)

1820

1820   Susan B. Anthony (below), a leader of the American woman suffrage movement, is born

1821 Named governor of Florida Territory

1823   Mexico becomes a republic

1824 Runs for president; none of the candidates wins a majority of the electoral votes; the U.S. House of Representatives elects John Quincy Adams president

1826   The world's first photograph is taken by French physicist Joseph Niépce

JACKSON'S LIFE

WORLD EVENTS

Presidential Election Results:	Popular Votes	Electoral Votes
1828 Andrew Jackson	647,286	178
John Quincy Adams	508,064	83

1830

Congress passes the Indian Removal Act, forcing Native Americans to leave their homelands in the East for what is now Oklahoma — **1830**

1829   The first practical sewing machine is invented by French tailor Barthélemy Thimonnier (above)

1831   Young naturalist Charles Darwin goes to South America and the Galapagos Islands

Presidential Election Results:	Popular Votes	Electoral Votes
1832 Andrew Jackson	687,502	219
Henry Clay	530,189	49

The South Carolina legislature tries to nullify tariffs passed by the U.S. Congress; the state is forced to back down — 1832

Fights the power of the Second Bank of the United States — 1832–1836

1833   Great Britain abolishes slavery

JACKSON'S LIFE

The U.S. government   1835
is out of debt for
the first and only
time in history

Returns home   1837
to the Hermitage
(below), near Nashville

June 8, dies at home   1845

1840

WORLD EVENTS

1835-   Texas fights a war
1836   to gain independence
from Mexico

1837   American banker J. P.
Morgan is born

1840   Auguste Rodin,
famous sculptor of
The Thinker, is born
in France

1848   *The Communist
Manifesto,* by German
writer Karl Marx
(above), is widely
distributed

UNDERSTANDING ANDREW JACKSON AND HIS PRESIDENCY

★ ★ ★

IN THE LIBRARY

Judson, Karen. *Andrew Jackson.*
Berkeley Heights, N.J.: Enslow, 1997.

Parlin, John. *Andrew Jackson: Pioneer and President.*
Broomall, Pa.: Chelsea House, 1991.

Whitelaw, Nancy. *Andrew Jackson: Frontier President.*
Greensboro, N.C.: Morgan Reynolds, 2001.

ON THE WEB

For more information on *Andrew Jackson*, use
FactHound to track down Web sites related to this book.

1. Go to *www.facthound.com*
2. Type in this book ID: 0756502551
3. Click on the Fetch It button.

Your trusty FactHound will fetch the best Web sites for you!

JACKSON HISTORIC SITES
ACROSS THE COUNTRY

Chalmette Battlefield and National Cemetery
8606 West Saint Bernard Highway
Chalmette, LA 70043-4204
504/281-0510
To learn more about Jackson's
victory at the Battle of New Orleans

The Hermitage
4580 Rachel's Lane
Nashville, TN 37076-1344
615/889-2941
To visit Jackson's home and burial site

Horseshoe Bend National Military Park
11288 Horseshoe Bend Road
Daviston, AL 36256-9751
256/234-7111
To visit the site of Jackson's defeat of the Creeks

THE U.S. PRESIDENTS
(Years in Office)

★ ★ ★

1. **George Washington**
   (March 4, 1789-March 3, 1797)
2. **John Adams**
   (March 4, 1797-March 3, 1801)
3. **Thomas Jefferson**
   (March 4, 1801-March 3, 1809)
4. **James Madison**
   (March 4, 1809-March 3, 1817)
5. **James Monroe**
   (March 4, 1817-March 3, 1825)
6. **John Quincy Adams**
   (March 4, 1825-March 3, 1829)
7. Andrew Jackson
   (March 4, 1829-March 3, 1837)
8. **Martin Van Buren**
   (March 4, 1837-March 3, 1841)
9. **William Henry Harrison**
   (March 6, 1841-April 4, 1841)
10. **John Tyler**
    (April 6, 1841-March 3, 1845)
11. **James K. Polk**
    (March 4, 1845-March 3, 1849)
12. **Zachary Taylor**
    (March 5, 1849-July 9, 1850)
13. **Millard Fillmore**
    (July 10, 1850-March 3, 1853)
14. **Franklin Pierce**
    (March 4, 1853-March 3, 1857)
15. **James Buchanan**
    (March 4, 1857-March 3, 1861)
16. **Abraham Lincoln**
    (March 4, 1861-April 15, 1865)
17. **Andrew Johnson**
    (April 15, 1865-March 3, 1869)

18. **Ulysses S. Grant**
    (March 4, 1869-March 3, 1877)
19. **Rutherford B. Hayes**
    (March 4, 1877-March 3, 1881)
20. **James Garfield**
    (March 4, 1881-Sept 19, 1881)
21. **Chester Arthur**
    (Sept 20, 1881-March 3, 1885)
22. **Grover Cleveland**
    (March 4, 1885-March 3, 1889)
23. **Benjamin Harrison**
    (March 4, 1889-March 3, 1893)
24. **Grover Cleveland**
    (March 4, 1893-March 3, 1897)
25. **William McKinley**
    (March 4, 1897-
    September 14, 1901)
26. **Theodore Roosevelt**
    (September 14, 1901-
    March 3, 1909)
27. **William Howard Taft**
    (March 4, 1909-March 3, 1913)
28. **Woodrow Wilson**
    (March 4, 1913-March 3, 1921)
29. **Warren G. Harding**
    (March 4, 1921-August 2, 1923)
30. **Calvin Coolidge**
    (August 3, 1923-March 3, 1929)
31. **Herbert Hoover**
    (March 4, 1929-March 3, 1933)
32. **Franklin D. Roosevelt**
    (March 4, 1933-April 12, 1945)

33. **Harry S. Truman**
    (April 12, 1945-
    January 20, 1953)
34. **Dwight D. Eisenhower**
    (January 20, 1953-
    January 20, 1961)
35. **John F. Kennedy**
    (January 20, 1961-
    November 22, 1963)
36. **Lyndon B. Johnson**
    (November 22, 1963-
    January 20, 1969)
37. **Richard M. Nixon**
    (January 20, 1969-
    August 9, 1974)
38. **Gerald R. Ford**
    (August 9, 1974-
    January 20, 1977)
39. **James Earl Carter**
    (January 20, 1977-
    January 20, 1981)
40. **Ronald Reagan**
    (January 20, 1981-
    January 20, 1989)
41. **George H. W. Bush**
    (January 20, 1989-
    January 20, 1993)
42. **William Jefferson Clinton**
    (January 20, 1993-
    January 20, 2001)
43. **George W. Bush**
    (January 20, 2001-)

INDEX

★ ★ ★

ABOUT THE AUTHOR

Barbara Somervill is a lifelong learner. Every project she undertakes provides her an opportunity to learn new information, understand a historical period, or develop an appreciation for life in other times.

She writes books, video scripts, magazine articles, and textbooks. One of her strangest subjects was a script about coffins!

Somervill grew up and went to school in New York. She received a bachelor's degree in English and a master's degree in education. She lives in South Carolina, is an avid reader and traveler, and enjoys movies and theater.